MW01710234

Without Sinning?

Joe Crews

Recently I read the amazing account of a man who submitted to a scientific hypnosis experiment. While under the influence of a light hypnotic trance the subject was ordered to pick up a glass from the table. Although he was a strong, athletic type, the man could not budge the glass from its position. His most strenuous exertions could not lift the glass that was light enough for any child to remove.

Why could he not do it? Because the scientists, after placing him in the trance, had told him that it was impossible to pick up the glass. Because his mind was convinced that it could not be done, his body was unable to carry out the command to lift it. What a dramatic demonstration that no person can really obey commandments which he believes to be impossible of performance!

Is this the reason so many Christians are living weak, defeated lives? There is no question that the popular, modern theology has been teaching millions that no one can really live without sinning. The Ten Commandments have been portrayed as an idealistic code produced only for the purpose of making people conscious of their need.

Many modern Christians are turning more and more to a soft, lenient stance on the subject of law-keeping. They believe God's love is incompatible with strict rules and penalties for violation.

That is a very comfortable doctrine but completely foreign to what the Bible teaches. Millions are being conditioned to break the great moral law of the universe—without feeling any guilt! The Word of God gives no one an excuse to feel relaxed about sin. It is the central problem of every person who has been born. Like a highly contagious disease, sin has infected every soul with the germs of death, and no earthly cure or deterrent has been found to halt the fatal progress of the sickness.

From the first appearance of sin in the Garden of Eden it has been totally disruptive of everything good. Never in one instance has it been able to coexist with righteousness and holiness. The requirements of God make it utterly impossible for sin or disobedience to be a part of the Christian lifestyle. The new tolerance for it is not biblical in any sense of the word. Jesus came to save people from it; He came to destroy it. It will never enter into heaven. Our attitude toward it must be uncompromising.

There can be no question of making it more acceptable by diminishing the amount of it or changing its form. *It must be destroyed.* And the only means of eradicating it is by receiving the fullness of Jesus Christ and His grace into the life.

How strange it is that so many church members have now become apologetic for sin, as though it cannot be prevented from triumphing in the life of a Christian. How dare we misrepresent the power of God's grace in the gospel! Jesus has already defeated the devil, and no Christian should be intimidated by an inferior, defeated foe. We have no business justifying the transgression of the Ten Commandments.

It is serious enough to engage willfully in an act of sin, but it is infinitely more deadly to defend it as something which cannot be prevented. To say that victory is impossible is to deny the adequacy of the gospel and to negate a large portion of the inspired Scriptures. In addition, it adds support to the original charge of Satan against

God, and gives a paralyzing, false security to everyone who believes in it.

Often people are defensive of sin because they have not been able to stop doing it in their own strength. For example, when they can't stop smoking, they must find a rationalization for its presence in their lives. Instead of making the humiliating confession that they can't conquer it, they fabricate arguments that it really doesn't hurt them or that no one can be perfect. Or the popular, convenient doctrine that no one can really live without sin anyway.

It is probably safe to say that the majority of Christians today are resigned to falling short of the moral law. In fact, they are quite satisfied that God doesn't even expect them to fulfill that law completely, either in the flesh or in the spirit.

The effect of such a teaching is exactly what one would expect—multitudes of emotionally happy, but disobedient, church members who feel that any concern about keeping the commandments is nitpicking and legalistic.

What a delusive strategy of Satan! As the inventor of the doctrine, the evil one is simply supporting his ancient accusation that God was asking too much. He accused God of being unfair by requiring something that was impossible.

He was able to convince a third of the angels that God was unreasonable to expect obedience to His law, and he has been trying to make everybody else believe it since that time. Think about it for a moment, and the entire scheme begins to make a lot of diabolical sense. Satan knows that sin is the only thing that will keep anyone out of heaven. Since sin is the "transgression of the law," he had to perfect a plan to make people look lightly upon breaking the law and also cause it to appear unobjectionable (1 John 3:4). To make the idea acceptable to Christians, Satan actually was able to disguise it as a doctrine and foist it upon a compromised Christianity.

In every evangelistic crusade, we meet it in one form or another, usually at the point of the law and the Sabbath. The inconvenient claims of obedience are shrugged off with a "Well, nobody can keep the Ten Commandments anyway."

But the problem doesn't end there. Even Christians who have accepted the claims of the moral law are not too concerned about how well they fulfill it either. In a subtle way they have been affected by the prevalent belief that too much concern about obedience is a form of salvation by works. Incredibly, some seem to be so fearful of keeping the law too closely that they actually make provision to break it. By doing so they perversely comfort themselves for not being legalistic.

How could people committed to commandment-keeping ever come to such a confused contradiction within themselves? Exposure to a false concept of righteousness by faith is only part of the answer. Much of the problem is based upon human failure and weakness of the flesh. Because they found themselves stumbling in their efforts to be perfect, they finally concluded that it was impossible not to sin. From that point it was easy to start interpreting Bible texts to support their weak experience. Satan exploited the psychological bent of the human mind to rationalize, and soon they had developed a comfortable doctrine that accommodated their occasional deviations from the law. Consequently, most Christians today are resigned to an alternating experience of victory-defeat, victory-defeat. To them it is the approved lifestyle of normal Christianity.

But something is fearfully wrong with this position. In the first place, doctrine should never be based on feeling or human experience. It must be rooted in the plain, unequivocal teaching of the Word of God. It is true that Bible texts can be assembled which seem to support the doctrine of spiritual imperfection. We are assured that all have sinned, that the carnal mind is enmity against God, and that man's righteousness is as filthy rags. But all the verses about failure, sin, and defeat are in reference to the *unregenerate* experience of a person. There are literally scores of other texts which describe an opposite experience of total victory and sinless living. In every case they are referring to the Spirit-filled life of a converted, committed child of God.

This distinction must always be recognized in the reading of the Scripture. The gospel of Jesus Christ is the *power* of God unto salvation. His grace is stronger than all the concentrated forces of evil. Jesus came to save His people from their sin. No one who reads the sixth chapter of Romans intelligently can believe that the Christian is free to practice sin. Paul utterly devastates the doctrine that a believer should keep on falling into sin.

It is true that provision is made for cleansing *in case* sin is committed, but God's perfect plan made it possible for man to overcome every sin and to live a life of perfect obedience through Christ. In fact, the promises of the Bible are so clear and specific on this point that it is hard to get confused. No secret meaning or hidden reservation can be found in the myriad of texts which describe the victorious experience of the born-again child of God. And just because one may not have grown into that fullness of faith which brings constant victory, he should not, therefore, deny the power of God to give such deliverance. When Peter began sinking in the Sea of Galilee, it was not because God's plan or power had failed. Peter could have rationalized, like so many modern Christians, and said, "God didn't want me to walk on the water, and besides, it's impossible for anybody to do such a thing anyway." Like our first parents we still tend to place the ultimate blame on God when we fail to follow His plan of holy living.

Total Victory Promised

The Spirit of God seemed to anticipate the struggle many would pass through in accepting the biblical assurances of total victory. Consequently the inspired writers were moved to use almost fanatical language in describing the possibilities for overcoming sin. Superlative expressions are utilized which actually boggle the mind. Instead of saying we may be saved, the Bible says we can be "saved to the uttermost" (Hebrews 7:25). Instead of saying we may conquer, it assures that we can be "more than conquerors" (Romans 8:37). Instead of being told that we can just triumph, we are told that we may "always triumph" (2 Corinthians 2:14). Instead of promising whatever we might ask to help us in our spiritual battles, the Bible says He will give us "exceeding abundantly above all that we ask or think" (Ephesians 3:20). And the verse just prior to that one clearly guarantees that we may "be filled with all the fullness of God" (verse 19).

Admittedly, many of these promises are too vast for our human minds to comprehend fully, but surely they are intended to impress us with the magnitude of God's resources in our behalf. If the language sounds exaggerated it is only because we are too feeble in faith and too weak in the flesh to believe such purity and sanctification could ever be fulfilled in us. We tend to trust our feelings quicker than the Word of God.

Is it important to believe the promises exactly as they read? Yes, because it is only through those promises that deliverance can be accomplished. "Whereby are given unto us exceeding great and precious promises: that by these ye might be partakers of the divine nature, having escaped the corruption that is in the world through lust" (2 Peter 1:4).

Notice that it is "by these" that we escape the corruption of sin. What are "these"? The promises of God. The sequence of victory is plainly marked out in this fantastic text. By faith in the promise we become a partaker of the divine nature, and through the power of that new nature in us we are able to escape the corruption of sin. In other words, everything depends on the surrender and commitment of one's self to the indwelling Spirit of Christ. "Without me," Jesus said, "ye can do nothing" (John 15:5).

Equally important is the inspired comment of Paul, "I can do all things through Christ which strengtheneth me" (Philippians 4:13). That little expression "all things" is the key to victory for every one of us. It includes power over drugs, immorality, appetite, pride, and every act of sin that would rob us of eternal life.

All Things Available

The big point here is that when you get the power of Christ in your life, you have everything else you could ever desire. "He that spared not his own Son, but delivered him up for us all, how shall he not with him also freely give us all things?" (Romans 8:32). There is that term again—"all things." You will find it also in 2 Peter 1:3: "According as his divine power hath given unto us all things that pertain unto life and godliness ..."

When you put those texts together, an incredible picture emerges. By claiming the presence of Christ in your life, you also receive everything that Christ possesses. Paul described it this way: "But of him are ye in Christ Jesus, who of God is made unto us wisdom, and righteousness, and sanctification, and redemption" (1 Corinthians 1:30).

Here the "all things" are broken down into very particular, individualized experiences, and we begin to see that Peter was right in stating that God has given us all things that pertain to godliness. Those Christians who doubt the possibility of overcoming sin completely should read these verses carefully. What do those words "righteousness," "redemption," and "sanctification" include? All three of those words promise us more than deliverance from the guilt of our past sins. The word "redemption" is not limited to redemption from the guilt of sin, but from the power of sin also. "Sanctification" is a word that describes continuous, daily growth in overcoming sin. "Righteousness" literally means right-doing and applies to a dynamic fulfillment of God's will. They are all big words, but they all have the connotation of being set free, both from the guilt and the practice of sin.

Every child of Adam needs two things desperately—forgiveness for the past, and power for the future. Redemption includes both of them; and the idea that *full* deliverance from the guilt of sin is included, but only *partial* deliverance from the power of sin, is a perversion of the gospel. Jesus did not come to save us from the consequences of sin only, but to save us from the sin itself. Salvation is not a negative thing; not just the absence of something. He did not come just to take away something—our guilt—but to give us something—victory over sin. For God to forgive us and leave us under the power of continued sin would make God an accomplice of sin. He not only *counts* us righteous through the imputation of His atoning death, but He *makes* us righteous through the impartation of His victorious life.

After thoughtfully reading the entire sixth chapter of Romans, if you need more assurance that victory can be yours, read the following:

- 1 Corinthians 15:57—"But thanks be to God, which giveth us the victory through our Lord Jesus Christ."
- 1 John 5:4—"For whatsoever is born of God overcometh the world: and this is the victory that overcometh the world, even our faith."
- Philippians 2:5—"Let this mind be in you which was also in Christ Jesus."
- 2 Corinthians 5:21—"… that we might be made the righteousness of God in him."
- 1 John 3:6—"Whatsoever abideth in him sinneth not: whosoever sinneth hath not seen him, neither known him."

Let us return for a moment to the analogy of the hypnotized man. He could not physically lift a small glass from the table because his mind was so fully convinced that it couldn't be done. Has Satan been able to immobilize the church through the power of his hypnotic, lying assertion that obedience is impossible? It certainly seems so.

No one is going to put forth any serious effort to do something that he believes to be impossible. Obviously then, those who believe they cannot live without sinning are not attempting to live without sin. No reasonable person will waste time and effort in a vain struggle to accomplish nothing.

That brings us to an interesting question: Can a person believe that there is no way to stop sinning, and yet make plans not to sin? Logically, it would seem highly unlikely, if not impossible. Yet the Bible commands us to "make not provision for the flesh, to fulfill the lusts thereof" (Romans 13:14). Do we indeed make provision for sin by holding that it is impossible not to sin?

To Him That Overcometh

The entire book of Revelation is addressed to the seven churches of Asia. In each of the churches certain ones received high commendation and glorious promises of heavenly reward. Without exception the blessing was extended "to him that overcometh." Those seven churches symbolize every period of the Christian church from the apostles to the end of time. If victory over sin is not possible, no soul will be saved from those centuries of time.

To deny the possibility of total victory over sin is to rob God of the glory of His mission. He came, the Bible says, to destroy the works of the devil. Those works are the works of sin. If no one claimed His power to overcome sin completely, the devil's accusation would be confirmed. The requirements of God would be exposed as too difficult to obey.

Jesus stated that He had comc "to seek and to save that which was lost" (Luke 19:10). Here He indicated that more than just people needed to be restored. "That which was lost" included a sinless character. His mission was to counteract and neutralize the entire program of sin-defilement introduced by Satan. Restoring the image of God in man is a very important part of the everlasting gospel. That work of the gospel must be done before Jesus comes and not as some magical afterthought of our returning Lord.

The book of Revelation identifies the crowning characteristic of the redeemed as obedience. "Here is the patience of the saints: here are they that keep the commandments of God, and the faith of Jesus" (Revelation 14:12). "And the dragon was wroth with the woman and went to make war with the remnant of her seed, which keep the commandments of God, and have the testimony of Jesus Christ" (Revelation 12:17). "Blessed are they that do his commandments, that they may have right to the tree of life, and may enter in through the gates into the city" (Revelation 22:14).

How significant it is that man's condition for remaining in Eden is also the condition for being restored to Eden. Anyone who believes obedience is unimportant should read again the dramatic story of Adam and Eve. A tiny, physical act of sin led to all the stark tragedy of the past 6,000 years. Those who are restored to that lost paradise will have demonstrated that they can be trusted with eternal life. Through faithful obedience in the face of death, they will have proven Satan's charges to be utterly false. Their steadfast loyalty will be an eternal guarantee of the security of God's restored dominion.

What can we say, then, concerning those who look so lightly upon the good works of obedience? They are subjects of grave deception and are playing into Satan's deadly sin-trap. The most glorious experience of the truly converted is to break the pattern of self-indulgence and sin. Under the rule of the Spirit of God, fleshly habits may be conquered and expelled from the life. Through faith in the promises unbelievable power may be released into the life of one who is willing to give up the enjoyment of sin.

The heart of God longs for us to take Him at His word and to claim the power He has promised. It is the only road to real victory. But no one can experience victory who does not believe victory is possible. Read again the assurances of the Bible. Do not try to twist them to match the weaknesses and failures of your human experience. They mean what they say. Deliverance is yours for the believing and the asking.

Right here we need to pause and consider an objection which is always brought against those who believe in total victory. It goes something like this: If you believe it is possible to live without sinning, are you able to say that your own life is free from sin?

Although the question deserves an answer, it should be pointed out that the objection is not relevant to the issue. If the Bible establishes a truth, it should be received on the grounds of its inspired authority and not on the basis of the messenger's experience. If victory over all sin is possible through Christ, it is true, whether the preacher has claimed it or not claimed it. Further, the work of sanctification is a progressive, lifelong experience and can never be considered as finished in point of time. Even if one could be unconscious of any known sin, he could never boast of being sinless. In fact, the person who is closest to perfection would surely be the least likely to recognize it. Because the nearer he gets to Jesus the more imperfect he will appear in his own eyes.

The claim might also be made that the doctrine of victory over sin is highly idealistic and too theologically complicated to be practical. But nothing could be farther from the truth. Even a child can understand the simple faith-transaction of appropriating the promises of the Bible. There is not a habit or sin known to man that cannot be conquered through faith.

In the next few minutes you will be able to appreciate the beauty of this divine victory plan. You will learn how to stop smoking, cursing, overeating, gossiping, or committing any other sin. Let nothing distract you as you proceed to the next paragraph. It could be the turning point of your life and mean more than all the money in the world. Since so many are struggling with cigarettes, I will use that indulgence as an illustration of the victory we are describing. Put your own problem into the text, and then take the four steps to glorious victory.

The Secret of Victory

Have you heard about the evolutionary way of getting the victory over tobacco, or any other sin? It is sometimes called the "tapering" method, but generally it just doesn't work. Oh, it partially works, of course, because old age takes care of some temptations and sins, and time settles the rest when death comes. But do you know why "trying" does not work in overcoming the devil?

Why can't we fight the devil for a few months and finally drive him away? Because the devil is stronger than we are. We could fight him for a year, but he would still be stronger than we are at the end of the year. Trying will never break the power of sin in a single instance, because we're facing an enemy who will always be stronger than we are. What, then, is the answer to our weakness and defeat? This question leads us to the sweetest and most sublime secret in the Word of God. Let us study it thoughtfully and with much prayer.

First of all, one must understand that all of heaven's gifts are available to us through the promises of the Bible, and we receive them by faith. Peter describes the "exceeding great and precious promises" and assures us that "by these ye might be partakers of the divine nature" (2 Peter 1:4). Mighty power is stored within the promise to fulfill itself to all who claim it in faith. So few are willing to believe that the promised blessing becomes theirs the very moment they believe it. Why is it so hard to believe implicitly that God will do what He promises?

Now let us come down to the very heart of victory and consider the four simple scriptural steps that any believer may take in claiming God's power. Four texts will illuminate the amazing transaction. *First:* "But thanks be to God, which giveth us the victory through our Lord Jesus Christ" (1 Corinthians 15:57). Allow your mind to savor the fantastic message of these words. *Victory is a gift!* We do not earn it by our efforts, or deserve it because of any supposed goodness. The only thing we need do is ask for it, and the victory will be given to us freely by Christ. He is the only one who has ever gained the victory over Satan, and if we ever possess the victory, it will have to come as a gift from Him.

Let me ask you something. Do you need victory in your life over some binding, miserable habit of sin? Some are slaves to appetite, to alcohol, or tobacco. Others are struggling helplessly against impurity, anger, or worldliness. The Bible says you may have the victory as a gift through Jesus Christ. Do you believe He will give you that power if you ask Him? How certain can you be that God will answer your prayer for victory immediately? Here is how sure you can be—just as sure as Christ's words are true! Our *second* text is Matthew 7:11, "If ye then, being evil, know how to give good gifts unto your children, how much more shall your Father which is in heaven give good things to them that ask him?"

Is it a good thing when you ask for victory over tobacco, or any other fleshly or moral evil? Of course it is! And you don't even have to ask if it is God's will! He has already told us in the Bible that it is His will to destroy the works of sin and the devil. If we pray for more money or a better job we should always ask according to His will, but the victory over sin is promised to every one who asks in faith.

Will God give the victory when we ask Him? Jesus said He was more willing to give this good thing than we are to feed our children when they are hungry. He is waiting to honor your faith and to "supply all your need according to his riches in glory by Christ Jesus" (Philippians 4:19). These assurances are so open-ended and unlimited that our minds are staggered by it. Why have we been so reluctant to apply for the provisions of grace? Why is it so hard to believe that God means exactly what He says? He will keep every promise.

Faith Makes It So

Here is the next question. How do we know we have the victory after we ask Him? Simply because He said we would have it. We know God did not lie. We can believe His promise. The very moment we ask, we should accept the fact of fulfillment, thank Him for the gift, and get up and act like it has been done. No kind of proof-feeling or sign should be demanded or expected. The self-fulfilling power in the promise is released in response to our faith alone.

This brings us to the *third* text, found in Romans 6:11, "Likewise reckon ye also yourselves to be dead indeed unto sin, but alive unto God through Jesus Christ our Lord." The word "reckon" means to believe, or to consider it done. Every particle of faith should be focused on that one request for victory and then it should be accounted as done. Do you remember how Peter walked on the water? He asked Jesus if he could step out of the boat onto the raging sea, and Jesus told Peter to come. But how long did Peter do the impossible by walking on the water? The Bible says, "When he saw the wind boisterous, he was afraid; and beginning to sink, he cried, saying, Lord, save me" (Matthew 14:30).

What was Peter afraid of? He was afraid of sinking and drowning. In spite of Christ's assurance that he could safely walk on the water, Peter began to doubt the word of the

Master. That is when he began to sink. As long as he believed the promise of Jesus and acted in faith, he was safe. When he doubted, he sank.

Now, what is the impossible thing as far as you are concerned? It is not walking on water. It is overcoming that tobacco habit. And Christ says, "Come to me. I will give you the victory." As long as you believe that you have been delivered, you will have the victory. It is as simple as that. The very moment you ask for victory it will be placed in your life as a reservoir of power. You won't feel it, but it is there. It will remain there as long as you accept it in faith.

For some people the deliverance is so dramatic that they lose even the appetite for the sin. Tobacco addicts have sometimes been delivered from the craving, *but this is not the usual way God does it.* Usually, the desire remains, but in the moment of temptation, the power to walk past the temptation springs forth from within. Faith accepts the fact of deliverance and constantly claims the victory which is in the secure possession of the believer.

The final step to victory is described in our *fourth* text, Romans 13:14. "But put ye on the Lord Jesus Christ, and make not provision for the flesh, to fulfil the lusts thereof." So strong is the confidence in the appropriated power of God that no consideration is given to falling under the power of that sin again. Under the old "trying" plan, provision was made to fail in most cases. Cigarettes were placed on a shelf, and the smoker said to himself, "I'm going to try never to smoke again, but if I don't make it I know where they are." But under the "trusting" plan, we have no reason to fear failure on the grounds of human weakness. Victory does not depend on our strength but on God's power. We might fail, but He cannot fail. Cigarettes are thrown away. All plans that might involve any degree of compromise are abandoned.

Little Jimmy was in trouble because he had gone swimming against his mother's orders. When asked why he had disobeyed her, Jimmy answered, "Because I got tempted." Mother then said, "I noticed that you took your bathing suit with you this morning. Why did you do that?" Jimmy answered, "Because I expected to get tempted." How typical of those who do not quite trust their own strength to win the victory. They make provision to fail. They take their bathing suit along. With God there need be no provision to fail.

Someone might raise the objection that this could be discouraging. Suppose the person does fail? Even Peter began to sink. Would it not shake confidence in God if the victory was not maintained? No. Peter's sinking had nothing to do with the failure of divine power. It did not change Christ's will for him to walk on the water. It only pointed out Peter's need of stronger faith to enable him to obey Christ's command. Our faith could weaken. We might need to be reminded of our total dependence upon His strength. But this does not diminish the beautiful plan of God to impart power and victory through "exceeding great and precious promises" of the Bible. Without faith by the receiver not even God's promises can be appropriated. The limits are clearly defined in the words of Jesus, "According to your faith be it unto you" (Matthew 9:29).

There it is, friend, in all of its simplicity. *And it works!* If you are willing to be delivered, it works. Nothing will help the one who is not willing to give up the cigarettes. But if you want it, it is there. *Victory, power, deliverance*—just reach out in faith and it is yours. Believe it and claim it this very moment. God wants you to be free.